E220191975

CW00433513

SHOW ME SCIENCE

MAGNETS

By

Emilie Dufresne

BookLife
PUBLISHING

©2019
BookLife Publishing Ltd.
King's Lynn
Norfolk PE30 4LS
All rights reserved.
Printed in Malaysia.

A catalogue record for this
book is available from the
British Library.

ISBN: 978-1-78637-797-5

Written by:
Emilie Dufresne

Edited by:
Madeline Tyler

Designed by:
Gareth Liddington

Photocredits:

Cover – Driodworker, ShadeDesign, Vitaly Art, AnutaBerg, maglyvi, Ksena Shu, Macrovector, 4 – Denis Maliugin, 8 – Vita Olivko, tsvetina_ivanova, liya Bolotov, Studio G, Jakinnboaz, 9 – Alexander Shatilov, StockSmartStart, 11 – Jane Kelly, 13 – Diego Ioppolo, rvlsoft, 14 – natashanast, pic0bird, Lucia Fox, Maquiladora, 15 – Volonoff, Iconic Bestiary, 16 – Artram, 17 – OK-SANA, 18 – stockakia, Meilun, 20 – NotionPic, 21 – VitalyVK, autovector, 22 – IMissisHope, Colorcocktail, Julia Babii.

Images are courtesy of Shutterstock.com. With thanks to Getty Images, Thinkstock Photo and iStockphoto.

All facts, statistics, web addresses and URLs in this book were verified as valid and accurate at time of writing.
No responsibility for any changes to external websites or references can be accepted by either the author or publisher.

Contents

Words that look like <u>this</u> can be found in the glossary on page 24.

What Are Magnets?

A magnet is an object that gives off a magnetic field. A magnetic field is an invisible <u>force</u> that has an effect on magnetic materials and other magnets.

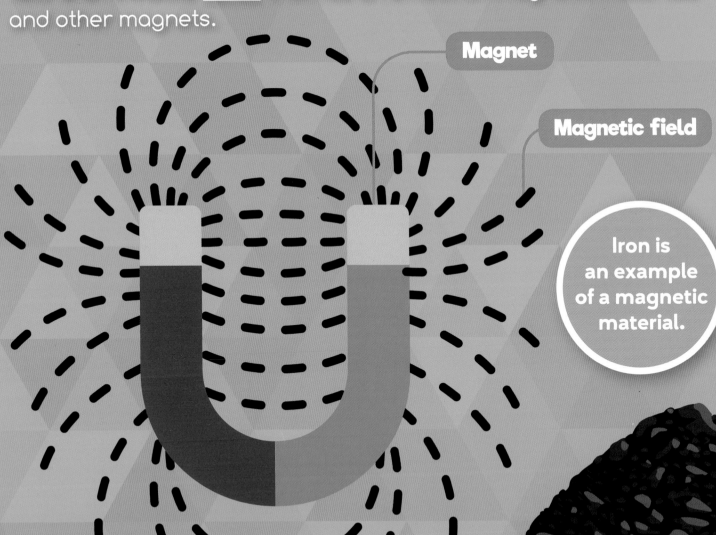

Magnet

Magnetic field

Iron is an example of a magnetic material.

4

Magnets can come in many different shapes and sizes. Here are a few of them.

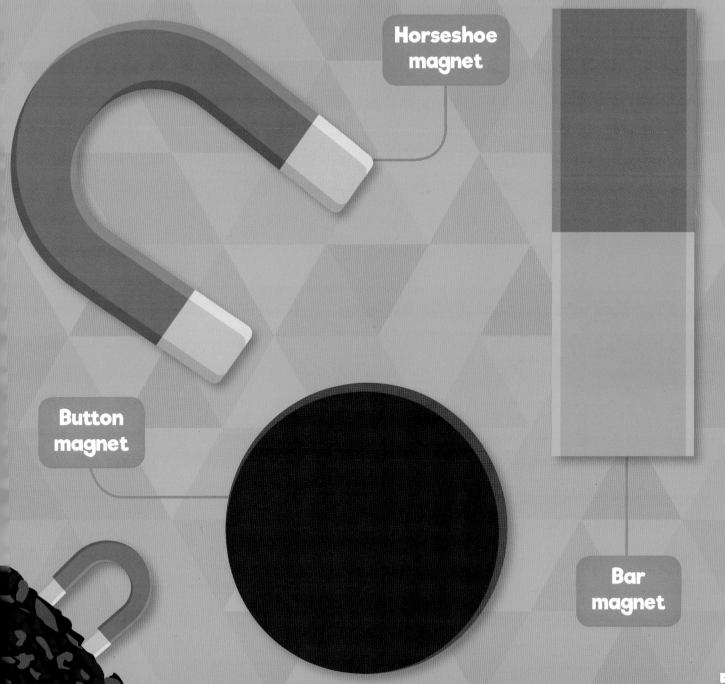

Horseshoe magnet

Button magnet

Bar magnet

What Do Magnets Do?

Magnets have the ability to attract or repel different objects, including other magnets. Attract means to bring closer. Repel means to push away.

These magnets are attracting each other.

S

N

N

S

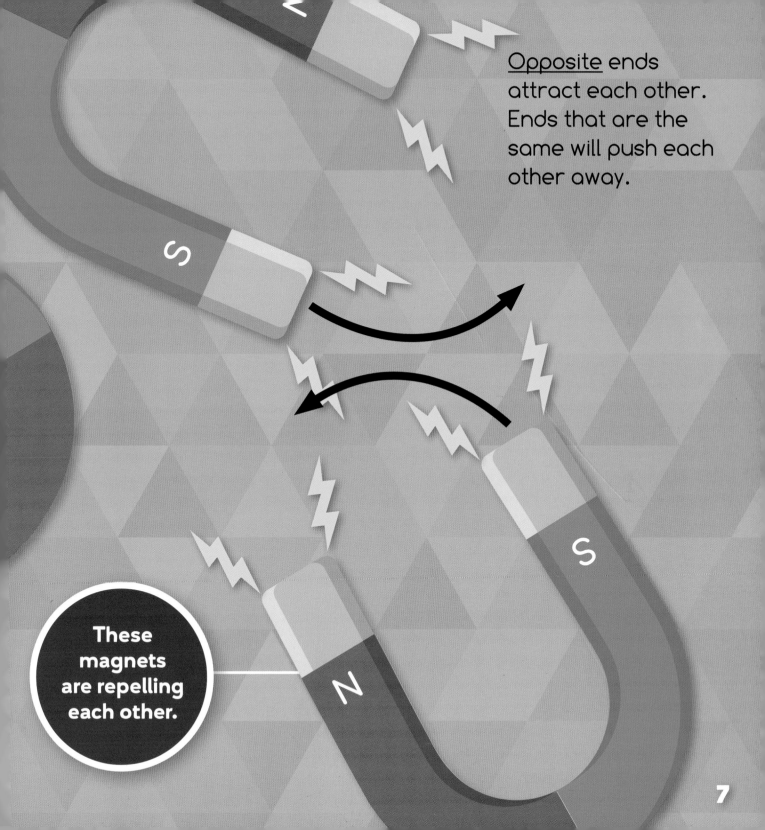

Opposite ends attract each other. Ends that are the same will push each other away.

These magnets are repelling each other.

How Are Magnets Used?

Magnets are useful because they can attract objects that aren't magnets. This means magnets can be used to do things such as picking up objects.

OBJECTS MAGNETS DO PICK UP

Metal cutlery

Screws

Metal paperclips

OBJECTS MAGNETS DON'T PICK UP

Pencil

Paper

Plastic toys

North and South Poles

There are two ends, or poles, to a magnet – the north and the south. North and south poles are attracted to each other.

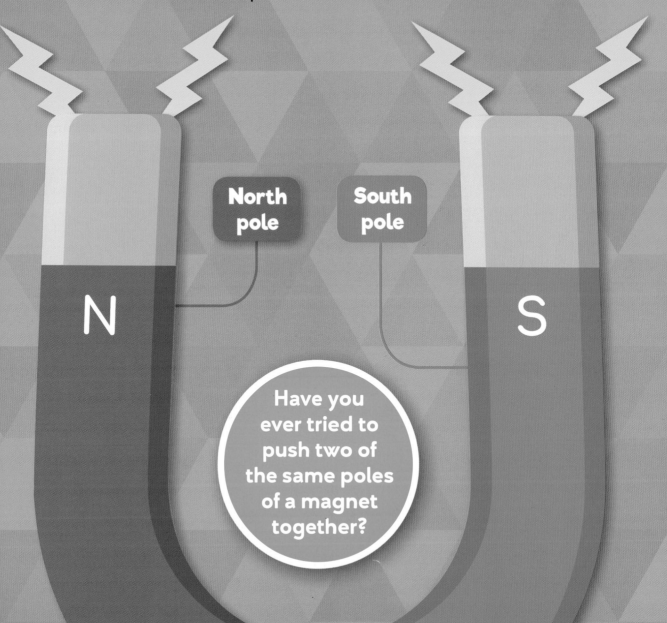

North pole

South pole

N

S

Have you ever tried to push two of the same poles of a magnet together?

The Earth acts like a giant magnet. This is how compasses work. Compasses have magnets inside which are attracted to the Poles of the Earth.

Find out more about compasses on page 17.

North Pole

South Pole

Magnet Patterns

Magnetic fields make very interesting patterns. The fields are invisible, so we need to do an <u>experiment</u> to be able to see them.

For this experiment, you will need:

A sheet of strong card

Iron filings

A magnet

STEP 1 - Hold the card at the edge.

STEP 2 - Pour the iron filings onto the card. Be careful not to spill any!

STEP 3 - Hold the magnet underneath the card so that it is touching the card.

STEP 4 - Move the magnet around underneath the card.

What happened to the iron filings as you moved the magnet around?

Magnets and Animals

Lots of animals use the Earth's magnetic field when <u>migrating</u>. Let's take a look at some of the animals that do this.

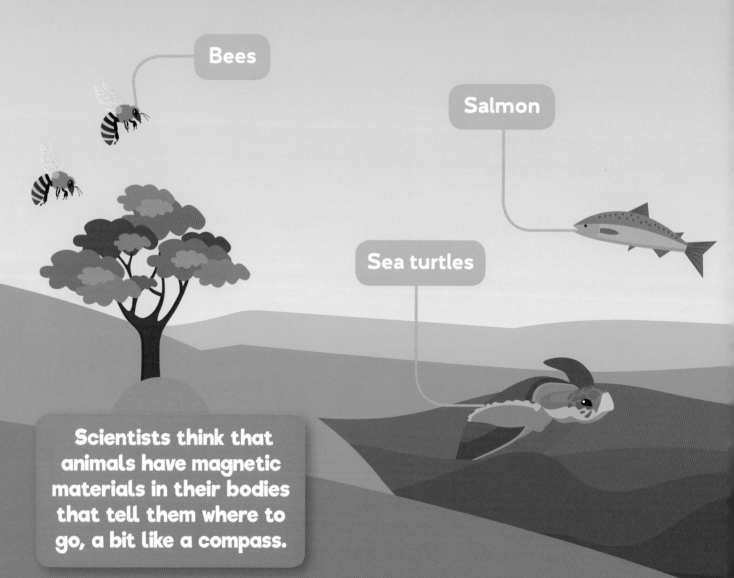

Bees

Salmon

Sea turtles

Scientists think that animals have magnetic materials in their bodies that tell them where to go, a bit like a compass.

Homing pigeons are also believed to have magnetic materials in their bodies. They are called homing pigeons because they can find their way home from a long way away.

The Earth's magnetism helps them do this.

Magnets in Nature

Lodestone is the strongest natural magnet found on Earth. They are magnetic rocks that were not made by humans.

If you find a rock that looks like this, why not test it with a metal object to see if it is magnetic?

Compasses use Earth's magnetic field to help us know which direction things are in: north, south, east or west.

This helps you find your way when you are somewhere with no <u>landmarks</u>, such as at sea or in a forest!

Discovering Magnets

The ancient Greeks believed that natural magnets at the bottom of the sea were powerful enough to pull ships to the bottom of the ocean. However, this is not true.

They also thought that magnets could be used to make people better if they were ill.

When a magnet, such as lodestone, is dangling from a string or sitting on a floating piece of wood, it points north, just like a compass. The name lodestone means 'the stone that leads'.

People in China invented a <u>marine</u> compass nearly 4,000 years ago!

Magnetic Inventions

There are lots of amazing inventions that use magnets. For example, metal detectors use magnets to help find when a metal is underneath the ground.

Maglev trains use magnets to <u>levitate</u>. The trains and the track are made from magnets that attract and repel each other. This means that the train floats above the tracks.

Speed (kilometres per hour)

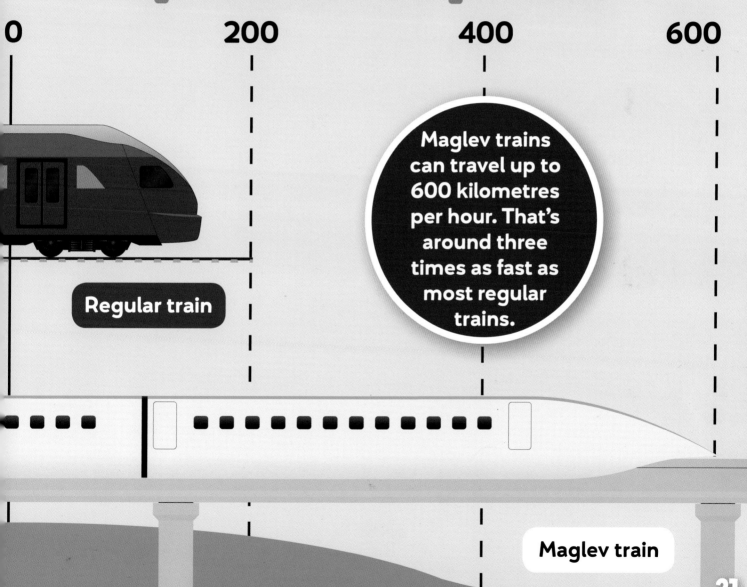

0   200   400   600

Regular train

Maglev trains can travel up to 600 kilometres per hour. That's around three times as fast as most regular trains.

Maglev train

Make Your Own Compass

Why not try and make your own compass?

To do this, you will need:

A metal needle

A magnet

A bowl of water

A cork

A compass

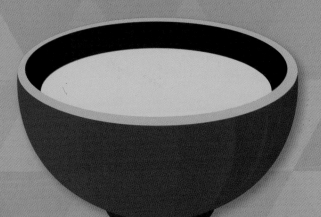

STEP 1 –
Rub the needle with the magnet 50 times. Make sure you stroke it in the same direction instead of back and forth.

STEP 2 –
Ask a grown up to push the needle through the cork.

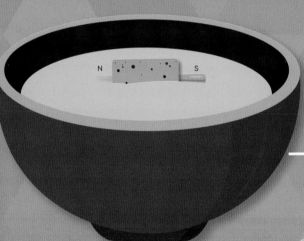

STEP 3 –
Place the needle and cork into the bowl of water and wait for it to stop turning.

STEP 5 –
Write down which way is north on your homemade compass and you're ready to go!

STEP 4 –
Use a compass to check your magnet is pointing north.

Glossary

experiment	a carefully planned test to find out something unknown
force	a push or pull on an object
landmarks	places or buildings that are easily recognised
levitate	float or hover in the air
marine	things relating to the ocean
migrating	when animals are moving from one place to another based on changes in the weather
opposite	two things which are completely different to each other

Index